JUL - - 2020

12 EPIC
RESCUES

by Samantha S. Bell

STORY LIBRARY

MORE TO EXPLORE

www.12StoryLibrary.com

12-Story Library is an imprint of Bookstaves.

Photographs ©: Eric Gay/Associated Press, cover, 1; arindambanerjee/Shutterstock.com, 4; Dieu Nalio Chery/Associated Press, 5; Richard Hartog/Associated Press, 6; Lionel Cironneau/ Associated Press, 7; Hugo Infante/Government of Chile/CC2.0, 8; Gobierno de Chile/CC2.0, 9; PD, 10; PD, 11; Lian Deng/Shutterstock.com, 12; Takeyasu Minamiura/minamiura. com, 13; Eric Gay/Associated Press, 14; Scott Rathburn/Associated Press, 15; Lutsenko_ Oleksandr/Shutterstock.com, 15; SDASM Archives/PD, 16; Frank Filan/Associated Press, 17; Jig Evil/Shutterstock.com, 18; Migren art/Shutterstock.com, 18; 2p2play/Shutterstock.com, 19; USCG/PD, 20; USCG/PD, 21; Star TV/YouTube, 22; Michele Cattani/Getty Images, 23; PD, 24; PD, 25; Marion Doss/CC2.0, 25; shrimpo1967/CC2.0, 26; PD, 27; Tagcaver2/PD, 28; Greg L/CC2.0, 29

ISBN
9781632357366 (hardcover)
9781632358455 (paperback)
9781645820222 (ebook)

Library of Congress Control Number: 2019938664

Printed in the United States of America
July 2019

June20
J
363.34

About the Cover
Rescue worker Steven Forbes carries baby Jessica McClure to safety after being trapped in a well in 1987.

Access free, up-to-date content on this topic plus a full digital version of this book. Scan the QR code on page 31 or use your school's login at 12StoryLibrary.com.

Table of Contents

Under the Rubble: The Rescue of Darlene Etienne

It was Tuesday, January 12, 2010. Sixteen-year-old Darlene Etienne was at her cousin's house in Port-au-Prince, the capital of Haiti. At 4:53 p.m. local time, a powerful earthquake with a magnitude of 7.0 struck near the city. The house came down on top of her. Etienne was trapped in a space just bigger than her body.

Etienne had been taking a shower when the earthquake hit. Because she was in the bathroom, she could get small amounts of water to drink.

But she had no food to eat. She could barely move. Etienne could hear people pass by. She screamed for help, but no one heard her.

Darlene Etienne poses with a photo of her rescue in 2011.

People from many countries came to help find survivors. They searched for many days. On January 23, Haiti's government called off the search. They thought all the survivors had been found. But the French workers kept looking.

On January 27, neighbors heard Etienne call out for help in a faint voice. She had been trapped under the rubble for 15 days. The neighbors contacted the authorities. A rescue team from France started digging her out. First, they created a hole big enough to give her food and water. Then they worked for 45 minutes to free her. She was covered in dust, but she was alive.

The French team gave her oxygen. They took her to a French medical ship. Etienne had a broken leg and was severely dehydrated, but she recovered. Many people believe it was a miracle that she survived.

3,000
Approximate number of people killed in the Haiti earthquake of 2010

- Darlene Etienne may have also had some cola to drink.
- Her pulse was weak when rescuers reached her.
- Rescuers believe she could have survived only a few more hours under the rubble.

5

Alone in the Storm: The Rescue of Abby Sunderland

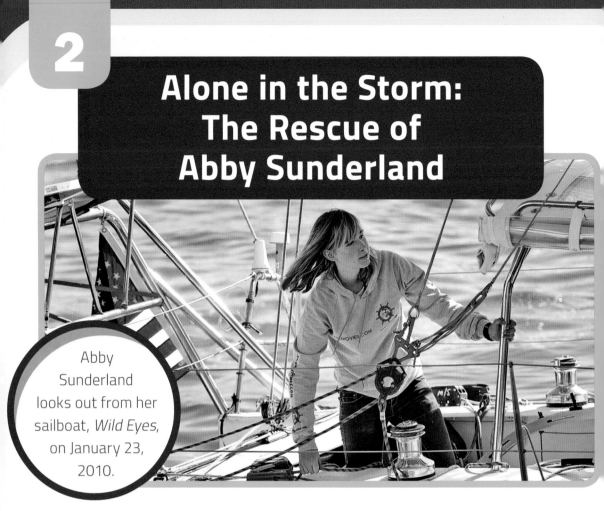

Abby Sunderland looks out from her sailboat, *Wild Eyes*, on January 23, 2010.

Sixteen-year-old American Abby Sunderland was already an experienced sailor. She wanted to become the youngest person to travel around the world solo and nonstop. On January 23, 2010, she left from Los Angeles, California, on her boat *Wild Eyes*. She kept in contact with her parents through satellite communications. But in May, her boat had problems. She had to stop for repairs in South Africa and lost her chance to set the record. She decided to finish the trip anyway.

Sunderland reached the Indian Ocean in June. But the stormy season had begun. On June 10, a huge wave hit *Wild Eyes* and broke the mast. It also knocked out the satellite communications.

Sunderland set off an emergency beacon. A massive rescue operation began. Ships from the United States, Australia, and France searched for

24

Hours it took the French boat to reach Abby Sunderland once she was found

- Many people criticized Sunderland's parents for letting someone so young go on such a dangerous trip.
- Sunderland's brother successfully completed a similar trip when he was 17.
- More than eight years later, *Wild Eyes* was found near Australia. It was covered in barnacles.

the teen. Rescuers chartered a jet. Late that day, the plane spotted the boat. Sunderland radioed the plane to let them know she had food and water.

Wild Eyes was badly damaged and had to be abandoned. The nearest vessel was a French fishing boat. Rescuing Sunderland wasn't easy. During the rescue, the captain fell into the water and had to be pulled out. Eventually, the crew got Sunderland to safety. But she had to leave everything behind.

THINK ABOUT IT

Sometimes things go wrong when sailing. These challenges can become even more dangerous when sailing alone. Do you think Sunderland's adventure was worth the risk? Why or why not?

Zac Sunderland reunites with his sister after her rescue by a French fishing boat.

The 33: The Rescue of the Chilean Miners

On August 5, 2010, 33 men were working in a copper mine in San Jose, Chile. Suddenly, the main ramp into the mine collapsed. The men were trapped 2,300 feet (701 m) underground. Within a few hours, rescuers arrived. Then another cave-in blocked their path. News about the men spread, and more help came. Some people searched for the men. Others worked on how to get them out.

About two weeks later, rescuers lowered a probe into the mine. When they pulled it back up, they found a note from the miners. The note said they were all fine. They were surviving on small amounts of tuna and water. By the next day, rescuers could communicate with them and send them more supplies.

Rescue efforts required the use of three different drills. NASA engineers

The capsule that was used to bring up the trapped miners.

Luis Urzúa (left), the leader of the trapped miners, was the last to be lifted out.

created a special capsule for the miners to ride in as they came to the top. The capsule would be slowly lowered and raised with a giant crane.

On October 9, one of the drills broke through the roof of the mine. Four days later, around midnight, the capsule came up with the first miner. After 22½ hours, all 33 miners had been brought to the top.

69
Days the miners were underground

- The miners ranged in age from 18 to 63.
- As rescuers drilled the holes, the miners had to clear away the rock.
- Approximately 1 billion people around the world watched the rescue live on TV.

MESSAGES FROM BELOW

While they were trapped, the miners recorded videos for their families. On August 26, they sent a message thanking their families for trying to free them. Two weeks later, they made another video showing their families what their day was like underground. It showed that they were still in good spirits.

Shipwrecked at Sea: Saving Lives on the *Andrea Doria*

On July 25, 1956, after eight days at sea, an Italian ocean liner named the *Andrea Doria* was nearing New York City. It had just entered the busy sea-lanes of the Atlantic off the US coast. By around 10:30 p.m., a Swedish passenger liner called the *Stockholm* was heading right for the *Doria*.

A thick fog blocked any view, so both captains depended on their radars.

Both radars showed another ship was coming. But one of the crew members on the *Stockholm* misread his radar. Around 11:10 p.m., the lights of both ships shone through the fog. It was too late to avoid disaster. The *Stockholm* rammed into the side of the *Doria*, creating a massive hole.

The captain of the *Doria* ordered the passengers and

A lifeboat of passengers being rescued, with the *Doria* listing in the background.

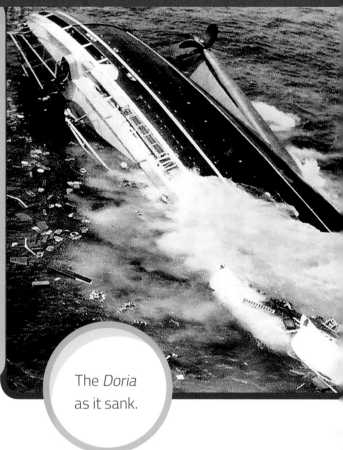

100

Number of times the *Andrea Doria* safely crossed the Atlantic before the collision

- The sinking of the *Doria* was one of the first televised tragedies.
- It ended the era of luxury cruise liners.
- The captain of the *Doria* never commanded another ship.

The *Doria* as it sank.

crew to abandon ship. But the lifeboats on the damaged side were no longer usable. The ships sent out distress calls for as many lifeboats as possible. At least 15 ships responded.

Some of the passengers died instantly. Debris from the crash trapped others in their cabins. Rescuers searched for survivors as the ship threatened to capsize. By 5:30 a.m., almost everyone had been evacuated. A few hours later, the *Andrea Doria* sank. Fifty-one people died, but about 1,660 were saved.

THE MOUNT EVEREST OF DIVING

A filmmaker once called the sunken *Andrea Doria* the Mount Everest of diving. The name stuck. The ship rests 240 feet (72.3 m) below the surface in international waters. Divers can find and keep small artifacts, such as pieces of china. Diving to the wreck can be dangerous. Help is miles away.

Trapped on Trango Tower: The Rescue of Takeyasu Minamiura

Trango Tower in Pakistan.

In August 1990, Japanese climber Takeyasu Minamiura climbed a new route up Trango Tower, a tall rock tower in Pakistan. Trango is 20,500 feet (6,248 m) high. The climb took 40 days. Minamiura planned to use a paraglider to drift back down, landing 6,000 feet (1,829 m) below on a glacier. On September 9, he attached all his food and equipment to a small parachute and released them to float down. But the bags hit a cliff and slid down instead.

When a good wind came around, Minamiura strapped on his paraglider and jumped. Right away, his chute hit the wall and collapsed. He slid down the tower's south face. Then his parachute snagged on a rock, stopping his fall. Minamiura was left dangling high in the air. All he had was a radio.

Minamiura called four of his friends. They had just finished their own climb on another rock tower nearby. As they planned a rescue, he spent the night in his paraglider. The next morning, he made his way to a narrow ledge.

Two friends hiked to a Pakistani army helicopter base. The pilots attempted a rescue, but it was too risky. The other two friends went to the other side of the Trango Tower. They made the dangerous climb to the top in just three days. They quickly rappelled to

Minamiura after his rescue from Trango Tower.

Minamiura's ledge and helped him down to the glacier below.

10

Days between Takeyasu Minamiura's jump and when he reached the glacier

- Pilots tried twice to drop food and water to Minamiura.
- On the second try, some cheese fell 15 feet above him.
- He risked the climb to get the cheese, his first food in six days.

THINK ABOUT IT

Minamiura had good friends. They did everything they could to help him. Think about your friends. Have you been able to help them in some way? How?

6

Everybody's Baby:
Saving Baby Jessica

On October 14, 1987, Jessica McClure was playing outside with four other children. She was 18 months old. The phone rang inside, and Jessica's mother went to answer it. Suddenly, the other children began screaming. Jessica's mother ran back outside. The toddler had fallen 22 feet (6.7 m) down a well in the backyard.

Jessica's mother called the police. They arrived in minutes. The well was only eight inches

(20.3 cm) wide. They could hear Jessica, but they couldn't see her. They lowered a video camera into the hole to find her. Then they sent down a microphone.

Rescuers brought in different kinds of digging equipment. They dug another deep hole beside the well. Then they drilled a horizontal tunnel between the two holes. It took a long time because they had to drill through rock. The tunnel was about two feet (0.6 m) below Baby Jessica.

Rescuers pumped oxygen into the well. But they couldn't give Jessica any food or water. They took turns staying by the well and talking to her. They could hear her cry and moan through the microphone. Sometimes she would sing songs like "Winnie the Pooh."

Finally, rescuers reached Jessica and brought her up. She had some injuries but eventually made a full recovery.

Workers use sound equipment to monitor Jessica's breathing.

24 HOURS A DAY

In 1987, CNN was the only 24-hour cable news network in the United States. It covered the rescue live. Millions of viewers watched the news day and night for updates. Jessica became known as "everybody's baby."

58
Hours Baby Jessica was trapped in the well

- Thousands of strangers sent her family toys, flowers, cards, and more.
- People donated approximately $1.2 million to Jessica.
- Today Jessica goes by her married name, Jessica McClure Morales. But her hometown still calls her "Baby Jessica."

7

Lost in Shangri-La: Saving the Survivors of the *Gremlin Special*

The Douglas C-47 was known as the *Gremlin Special.*

In May 1945, the United States was fighting Japan in World War II (1939–1945). Many Americans were stationed in the Pacific islands. The island of New Guinea had a hidden valley. The natives living there didn't know about the outside world. The Americans called the valley Shangri-La. Service men and women liked to go on airplane tours of Shangri-La.

On May 13, 24 Americans boarded a plane called the *Gremlin Special.* They were going to fly over the valley. The plane flew between the mountains to give the passengers a closer look. But clouds blocked the pilot's view. The plane crashed into the side of a mountain. Only two men and one woman survived. They had to walk for several days through the jungle to find an open area and get help.

40

Miles (64.4 km) from the crash site to Shangri-La

- Reporters were on the flights that brought supplies.
- A filmmaker came in on one of the flights.
- He parachuted into the valley to make a documentary about the rescue.

The three survivors (left to right): Sgt. Kenneth W. Decker, Cpl. Margaret Hastings, and Lt. John S. McCollon.

Rescuing the survivors would be difficult. Paratroopers could go into the valley, but there was no way to get them out again. A plane could not land safely. Helicopters couldn't fly high enough to go over the mountains. The paratroopers went anyway. Supplies were dropped in.

The only aircraft that could get back out of the valley were gliders. Rescuers sent gliders down. The paratroopers attached one end of a rope to the front of each glider.

They formed loops on the other ends and set them up on poles. Then the paratroopers and survivors strapped themselves into the gliders. Planes with hooks flew overhead. The hooks caught the loops and pulled the gliders back into the air and out of the valley.

Trapped in a Cave: The Rescue of the Wild Boars

Ekapol Chantawong coached a boys' soccer team in Thailand. The name of the team was the Wild Boars. On June 23, 2018, Chantawong took 12 team members into the Tham Luang Nang Non cave system. This is a popular tourist site.

But it was monsoon season. Rain fell while the team was inside, and the exit flooded. They moved further back into a cavern on higher ground. They ate snacks they had with them. They drank fresh water that dripped from a stalactite.

Outside, more than 3,000 rescuers from around the world came to help. On July 2, two British divers finally found the boys. But the water was

The view inside the Tham Luang Nang Non cave during the rescue.

THAILAND CAVE RESCUE

ENTRANCE

TEAM FOUND

4000 METERS

The
Wild Boars
soccer team at a
press conference
on July 18,
2018.

dark and muddy, and the boys didn't know how to swim. Over the next eight days, rescuers worked on a plan. During this time, divers brought the boys food and oxygen. One diver died as he was swimming back.

More rains were on the way, so rescuers had to hurry. Divers taught the boys how to swim with scuba gear. On July 8, the first four boys swam out, following a guide rope. Each boy had a diver in front and a diver in back. The rescue continued until July 10, when all the boys and their coach were safely out.

17
Days the Wild Boars were trapped in the cave

- The boys were ages 11–17.
- They had planned to stay in the cave for about an hour before coming out again.
- The only supplies the coach brought were a rope, spare batteries, and a flashlight.

GOOD FOR BUSINESS

Before the rescue, about 10 or 20 people would visit the cave each day. After the rescue, more than 6,000 came every day. Most of the visitors were from Thailand. They wanted to see where the rescue took place. Local residents made a lot of money selling snacks and souvenirs.

Sinking in a Storm: Saving the Crew of the *Sean Seamour II*

On May 2, 2007, three men set out to sail across the Atlantic. Jean Pierre de Lutz, Rudy Snel, and Ben Tye headed out to sea in a boat called the *Sean Seamour II*. On May 5, the weather started to change. By May 7, the boat was caught in Tropical Storm Andrea.

During the storm, winds reached 98 miles per hour (158 km/hr). The waves grew to 70 feet (21 m) high.

28
Minutes it took to complete the rescue

- The helicopter the Coast Guard used was called a Jayhawk.
- During the rescue, the raft drifted 1.8 miles (2.9 km).
- Before going back up, Dazzo put a hole in the raft and sunk it. That way, another crew wouldn't see it and attempt a rescue.

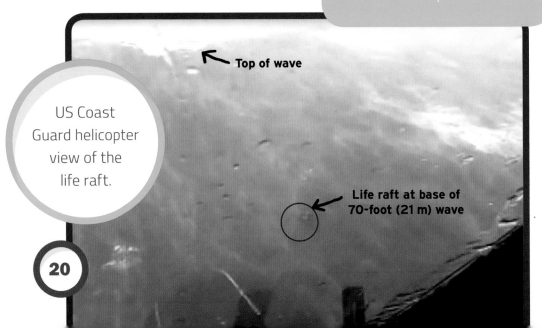

Top of wave

US Coast Guard helicopter view of the life raft.

Life raft at base of 70-foot (21 m) wave

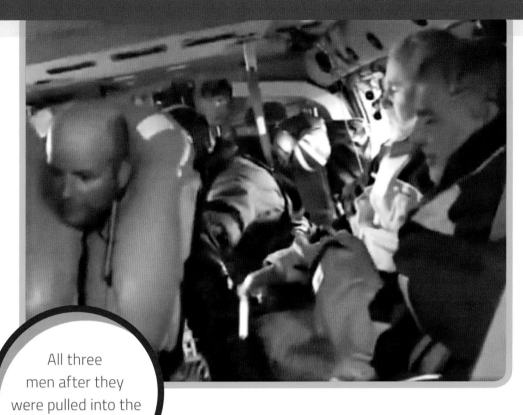

The *Sean Seamour II* was in big trouble. A device on board sent out a distress signal. The boat began to sink, and the three men climbed into the life raft. They struggled against the storm for six more hours.

Meanwhile, the distress signal had alerted rescuers. The Coast Guard sent a plane to find the men. The crew searched for the small black raft in the storm. They finally spotted it. The plane led a helicopter to the raft. The helicopter got into position 100 feet (30.5 m) above it. The winds were fierce.

As the helicopter hovered, a rescue swimmer named Drew Dazzo was lowered into the raging sea. Then the helicopter sent down a metal basket. Dazzo swam to the raft and saw that de Lutz was injured. He pulled de Lutz through the waves to the basket. De Lutz was lifted up to the helicopter. Dazzo went back to get the next man. When he went up in the basket, Dazzo returned for the last one. Then he fastened a hook to himself and went up, too.

Spider-Man in Paris: Climbing to Save a Child

In May 2018, a father in Paris, France, left his four-year-old son home alone to go shopping. While he was away, the boy went onto the balcony of their sixth-floor apartment. Somehow, he

fell over the railing. But on the way down, he grabbed hold of the edge of the balcony below. He hung on.

A crowd gathered, looking up at the boy. A migrant worker named Mamoudou Gassama saw him, too. Gassama was from Mali, a country in West Africa. He raced across the street and started to climb. He pulled himself up onto the balcony of the second floor. Then he stood on the railing and jumped, grabbing onto the balcony above him. With his feet dangling in the air, he pulled himself up to the third floor.

Gassama jumped again, now pulling himself up to the fourth floor. Meanwhile, another man grabbed onto the child's arm. But the man couldn't pull the little boy up.

Within moments, Gassama had reached the child. He grabbed the child's other arm and quickly lifted him back over the railing. He took

him back inside the apartment. Gassama started shaking and had to sit down. But the child was safe.

HONORING SPIDER-MAN

The mayor of Paris called Gassama "Spider-Man of the 18th," the district where the rescue took place. The Paris fire department praised his bravery. French President Emmanuel Macron rewarded Gassama with a certificate, a medal, and a job as a fireman. The president also gave him residency papers. In September 2018, Gassama became a French citizen.

22

Mamoudou Gassama's age in years when he rescued the child

- It took Gassama less than 30 seconds to reach the boy.
- Spectators took videos of the rescue and posted them on the internet.
- The boy's father was charged by police with child neglect.

23

Trapped Beneath the Sea: Rescuing the Crew of the USS *Squalus*

59
People on the *Squalus*

- While the crew members waited to be rescued, they tried to stay calm.
- They lay down, tried to nap, and didn't talk.
- They needed to preserve their strength and not use too much air.

The USS *Squalus* at the Portsmouth Navy Yard in January 1939.

On May 23, 1939, the submarine USS *Squalus* went underwater on a sea trial. It was near the coast of New Hampshire. But when the sub reached a depth of 60 feet (18 m), something went wrong. Minutes later, it began to flood inside. The submarine sank to the bottom of the ocean. The lower chambers filled with water,

and crew members in these areas didn't make it. Twenty-six men drowned.

But 33 men were still alive, trapped 243 feet (74 m) below the surface. Until that time, no submarine rescue attempt had ever succeeded. Lieutenant Commander Charles Momsen was called in. He had invented a diving bell for rescuing trapped submarine crews. A ship

The rescue diving bell is visible on the USS *Falcon* back deck.

called the USS *Falcon* brought Momsen's diving bell. The Navy sent their best divers.

Meanwhile, the crew of the *Squalus* sent up distress signals. Rescuers saw the signals and found the sub. Operations began to rescue the surviving crew members and one civilian. On May 24, the USS *Falcon* lowered the diving bell onto the hatch of the submarine. The survivors used the bell in groups of four. Thirteen hours later, the last ones reached the surface.

BREATHING UNDER THE SEA

Charles Momsen had friends who died in sunken submarines. He wanted to help keep that from happening again. Another of his inventions was the Momsen Lung. It was a breathing device that would allow a man to float up to the surface. The men on the *Squalus* had Momsen Lungs. They knew they had a chance to survive.

Back from the Dead: The Rescue of Lincoln Hall

Mount Everest is the highest mountain in the world. On May 25, 2006, Lincoln Hall made it to the top with his team. But on the way back down, Hall's brain began to swell from lack of oxygen. He started to hallucinate, and he could barely move. After about 10 hours, Hall collapsed in the snow. He was more than 29,000 feet (8,839 m) above sea level.

Native guides called Sherpas tried to revive him, but it was no use.

They kept trying for two hours, until sunset. When Hall still did not respond, they pronounced him dead. They had to go, or they would die, too. They took Hall's water, oxygen, and food.

The next morning, another team started on the last part of the climb. Around 7:30 a.m., they found Hall. But he wasn't dead. He was sitting near the edge of a cliff and changing his shirt. He

Aerial view of Mount Everest.

12

Hours Lincoln Hall was left for dead on the mountain

- Hall's team leader called his family and told them Hall had died.
- When the media began reporting he might be alive, people didn't tell the family in case it wasn't true.
- One of Hall's sons read the good news on the internet.

Lincoln Hall's book *Dead Lucky: Life After Death on Mount Everest* was published in 2008.

wasn't even wearing a hat or gloves.

Hall couldn't focus, stand, or speak clearly. He was shivering, and his fingers were frostbitten. The team gave him oxygen, water, and candy bars. Then they contacted Hall's group and waited with him for four hours until help arrived. It was too late for them to reach the top, but saving a life was worth it.

THINK ABOUT IT

Lincoln Hall was alone on a mountain, but he didn't give up. Describe a time when you didn't give up. Why did you keep trying?

More Epic Rescues

Human Chain Saves Drowning Family

In July 2017, six members of one family got caught in a rip current in the ocean off the coast of Florida. People on the beach rushed to form a line to reach them. About 80 people stretched out more than 100 yards (91 m), and the whole family was saved.

Rescued from America's Deepest Cave

Emily Davis Mobley was an experienced caver. In 1991, she was mapping a new section of Lechuguilla Cave in Carlsbad Caverns National Park. A rock fell and broke her leg 1,000 feet (304.8 m) underground. More than 200 rescuers maneuvered her up cliffs and through tight passageways to bring her to the top.

Heroes of the Hudson

In January 2009, pilot Chelsey "Sully" Sullenberger flew out of LaGuardia Airport in New York. The plane struck a flock of geese, damaging its engines. Sully turned the plane around and landed in the Hudson River. Police, firefighters, and medical crews boarded ferries. They rescued all 155 people on the plane.

Protected from Pirates

Captain Richard Phillips was piloting the *Maersk Alabama* to Kenya in April 2009. The ship was attacked by four Somali pirates. They took Captain Phillips hostage and held him on a small lifeboat for five days. Navy SEALS captured one of the kidnappers and shot the other three, saving Phillips.

Glossary

beacon
A guiding signal.

dehydrated
Having lost a large amount of water.

glider
An aircraft without an engine that glides on air currents.

hallucinate
To experience something that seems real but actually is not.

horizontal
Parallel with the ground.

migrant worker
A person who moves to another country to find seasonal or temporary work.

monsoon
Seasonal winds that blow between May and September and bring rain.

paraglider
A wide canopy resembling a parachute that allows a person to glide through the air.

paratrooper
A person trained to jump from an airplane using a parachute.

probe
A long, slender instrument used for exploring.

rappel
To move down a rock face by using a rope tied around the body and secured at a higher point.

stalactite
A pointed piece of rock that hangs like an icicle from the roof of a cave.

Read More

Otfinoski, Steven. *Captain Sully's River Landing: The Hudson Hero of Flight 1549*. North Mankato, MN: Capstone Press, 2019.

Scott, Elaine. *Buried Alive!: How 33 Miners Survived 69 Days Deep Under the Chilean Desert*. New York: Clarion, 2012.

Tougias, Michael. *A Storm Too Soon: A Remarkable True Survival Story in 80 Foot Seas*. New York: Henry Holt & Co, 2016.

Visit 12StoryLibrary.com

Scan the code or use your school's login at **12StoryLibrary.com** for recent updates about this topic and a full digital version of this book. Enjoy free access to:

- Digital ebook
- Breaking news updates
- Live content feeds
- Videos, interactive maps, and graphics
- Additional web resources

Note to educators: Visit 12StoryLibrary.com/register to sign up for free premium website access. Enjoy live content plus a full digital version of every 12-Story Library book you own for every student at your school.

Index

About the Author

Samantha S. Bell lives in upstate South Carolina with her family and lots of animals. She is the author of more than 100 nonfiction books for children.